IMAGES
of Aviation

THE
ROYAL NAVAL
AIR SERVICE

Winston Churchill, First Lord of the Admiralty, striding purposefully down Whitehall in 1915.

IMAGES
of Aviation

THE
ROYAL NAVAL
AIR SERVICE

Compiled by
Terry C. Treadwell and Alan C. Wood

TEMPUS

First published 1999
Copyright © Terry C. Treadwell and Alan C. Wood, 1999

Tempus Publishing Limited
The Mill, Brimscombe Port,
Stroud, Gloucestershire, GL5 2QG

ISBN 0 7524 1627 8

Typesetting and origination by
Tempus Publishing Limited
Printed in Great Britain by
Midway Clark Printing, Wiltshire

An excellent shot showing a Sopwith 2F1 Camel, No.N6779, aboard the cruiser HMS *Calliope*. This shot highlights the very short take-off runway the aircraft had.

Contents

Melvin Rattray taking off from HMS *Queen Elizabeth* in a Sopwith 1½ Strutter.

Acknowledgements

We would like to thank the following for all their assistance in helping us to obtain some of the photographs: Chaz Bowyer, Captain Ted Wilbur, USN, and John Batchelor. The majority of the photographs come from our own collection.

Introduction

At 2300 hours on 4 August 1914 the message 'COMMENCE HOSTILITIES AGAINST GERMANY' was flashed from the wireless room of the Admiralty in London to all ships of the Royal Navy. As far as the Royal Navy was concerned their part in the war was going to be a global sea struggle against the Imperial German Navy. Both protagonists had a powerful ocean-going array of warships in service and knowledge of the location of enemy ships was vital. Reconnaissance activity by aircraft to locate ships and communicate this information was the key and the newly formed Royal Naval Air Service was to play a crucial role.

The Royal Navy's interest in aviation began in 1908 when it was proposed to the Admiralty that a rigid airship be purchased and a new post of Naval Air Assistant be established. The airship *Nulli Secundus*, British Airship No.1, had flown over London on 5 October 1907 and around the War Office in Whitehall, creating quite a stir. The Admiralty saw the potential of such a craft, as they monitored the unrest in Europe and the rapid development of the German Zeppelins. They approached the shipbuilders Vickers, Son & Maxim, who had been building ships for the navy for a number of years, with a proposal for an airship. The company had never built anything remotely like an airship before, but nevertheless in 1909 they were given a contract for £35,000 and work began on the construction of Naval Airship No.1, the *Mayfly*. Two years later, on 22 May 1911, the *Mayfly* emerged from its building shed at Barrow-in-Furness, 512 feet long and 48 feet in diameter, and immediately had to ride out a gale whilst tied to her mooring mast. There were misgivings about the airworthiness of the airship from day one but it wasn't until 22 September 1911 that the navy was forced to accept it. While in the process of backing the *Mayfly* out of her shed, she was caught by a gust of wind and damaged beyond repair. This accident convinced the Admiralty that aeroplanes were more suitable than airships for a multi-use naval role.

The Royal Navy's interest in the use of aircraft on ships started not with anything that happened in Britain but in Virginia, USA. On Monday 14 November 1910 a civilian by the name of Eugene Ely, in a Curtiss pusher biplane, roared down a wooden ramp on board the American light cruiser USS *Birmingham*, swooping into the sky and into history. It was the first time an aircraft had flown from a ship. The Americans continued to carry out experiments with ships and aircraft and all the time Britain watched with increasing interest.

At the point when the *Mayfly* dampened the navy's enthusiasm for airships, trials of military aircraft had been being carried out by the British Army for two years, so the Admiralty decided to make use of this army experience and apply it to naval purposes. Three officers from the Royal Navy and one from the Royal Marines were sent to Eastchurch to be trained as pilots. Among the four pilots was a Lieutenant Charles Rumney Sansom, RN, who was to become one of the most influential pilots in the Royal Navy. Sansom was also a close friend of Winston Churchill, the First Lord of the Admiralty. He persuaded Churchill to have a flight and in 1912 he took to the air in a Short S.27 flown by Lt A.V. Longmore. Churchill was hooked, becoming an ardent supporter of naval aviation (his interest later culminated in him taking flying instruction and becoming a pilot himself).

Trials were carried out with a variety of different aircraft, predominantly seaplanes as these appeared to be the most natural progression of the aeroplane as far as the navy were concerned. The first experimental naval flight from a ship was made by Lt Sansom in a Short S.27 aircraft. On 10 January 1912 he took off from the deck of the cruiser HMS *Africa* to record a milestone in aviation history. On 9 May 1912 a second flight by a Short S.27 was made by a Lieutenant R. Gregory from a moving warship, HMS *Hibernia* in Weymouth Bay, Dorset. Both flights were successful and proved that aircraft could take off from ships. By the end of 1912 the Royal Navy had acquired sixteen aircraft – thirteen landplanes and three hydro aeroplanes (the term seaplane was not introduced until 17 July 1917).

Short Admiralty Type 827 No.3326, built by Brush Electrical Engineering, taking off from RNAS Calshot.

Before 1913 both the RFC and the navy had several airships but in 1913, when all airships came under the command of the Royal Navy, a Royal Naval Airship Service was formed. The Royal Naval Air Service (RNAS) was formed on 1 July 1914 from the naval wing of the Royal Flying Corps, formed 13 May 1912. The first wing of the RNAS was established at Eastchurch in September 1914, under the command of (by this stage) Wing Commander C.R. Samson, RN. Samson is credited with the idea of using armoured cars for ground patrols, out of which beginnings grew the Talbot and Lanchester armoured cars of the RNAS Armoured Car Division.

In 1914, as war clouds started to gather in Europe, the Royal Naval Air Service had ninety-three aeroplanes and seaplanes plus a mere seven non-rigid airships, all together crewed by 100 officers and 550 ratings at six air stations. When the First World War broke out, with Germany and the Austro-Hungarians as the main opponents, the Royal Navy, although possessing the largest and most powerful fleet of warships in the world, realised that the aircraft had its place in any forthcoming conflict as an observation platform. It was to become the eyes of the fleet.

When the signal to commence hostilities flashed to British forces, the navy moved to locate the position of the German fleet. However, the first contact with the enemy was not to be in Europe, but in Africa. The German light cruiser SMS *Königsberg* had fired upon the British cruiser HMS *Pegasus* off Zanzibar. *Pegasus* returned fire but was outgunned and sunk. HMS *Chatham* went to give battle but could not locate *Königsberg*, which had retreated into the delta of the Rufigi River in Tanganyika (now Tanzania).

HMS *Chatham* blockaded the mouth of the river to prevent the escape of *Königsberg* into the Indian Ocean, whilst Admiral King Hall in Durban enlisted a civilian pilot – H.D. Cutler – into the RNAS with the rank of Flight Sub Lieutenant. Cutler had a 90hp Curtiss flying boat which was impressed into RNAS service and on 19 November 1914 he went to find *Königsberg*. On 3 December Cutler found *Königsberg* twelve miles up river and radioed back to the Admiralty. Further flights were made by Cutler but on 10 December 1914 he was forced down by engine failure and taken prisoner. He remained so until November 1917.

The Admiralty decided to bomb *Königsberg* with two Sopwith Type 807 seaplanes. These proved unsuitable and were replaced by Short Type 827s which made an abortive reconnaissance mission.On 18 June 1915 two Henry Farmans and two GIII Caudrons arrived and on 6 July 1915 Flt. Lt J.T. Cull, flying a Farman, bombed *Königsberg* from 6000 feet with two bombs. These missed and the Farman was shot down, but fortunately the pilot was rescued. The Royal Navy then disposed of *Königsberg* by gunfire from the two shallow draft gunboats.

Back in England, three fast cross-channel ferry boats had been converted to seaplane carriers. The *Engadine, Riviera and Empress* were intended to compensate for the loss of the navy's only 'aircraft carrier', HMS *Hermes*. She had been sunk on 31 October 1914 in the Straits of Dover by the German submarine U-27. She was quickly replaced by HMS *Ark Royal*, a converted tramp steamer.

No. 1 Squadron, RNAS, were equipped with the Sopwith Tabloid and then posted to Ostend to patrol along the Channel and protect the British Expeditionary Force (BEF) from enemy aerial attack. The squadron were soon in action. On 22 September 1914 four bomb-carrying Sopwith Tabloids – piloted by Lts Gerrard, Marix, Spenser-Grey and Colet – carried out the first British air raid on Germany. Their target was the Zeppelin hangars at Düsseldorf but the mission was ineffective; only two bombs were dropped which failed to explode.

In October 1914 the RNAS established its first forward base at Antwerp then a second at Belfort, France. In the same month two aircraft, piloted by Squadron Commander Spenser-Grey and Flight Lieutenant Marix, attacked Zeppelin hangars at Düsseldorf and Cologne. Spenser-Grey's target at Cologne was clouded so he bombed his secondary target, a railway station, with limited success. Marix located his Düsseldorf target and dropped two 20lb bombs

RNAS cooks at Crystal Palace after completing a one-month course. They are lined up for kit inspection prior to going abroad to the Middle East.

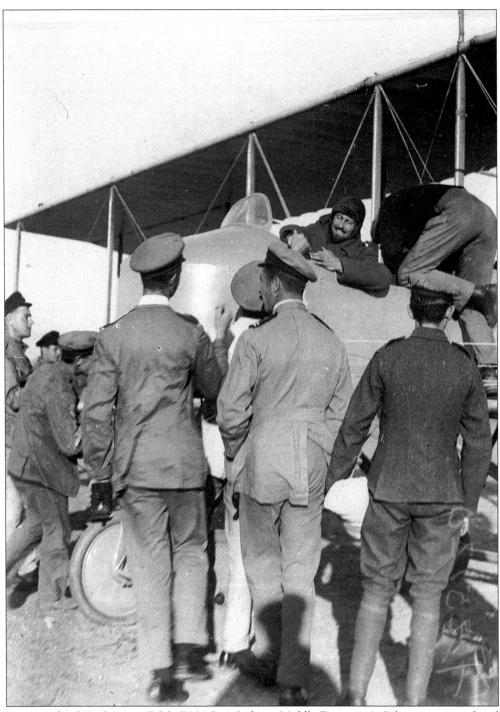

Commander C.R. Samson, DSO, RNAS, at Imbros, Middle East, in 1915, being congratulated on his return from a bombing sortie in his Voisin.

An excellent shot of Dundee Air Station taken from 2000 feet, showing the two slipways.

accurately from 600 feet. The Zeppelin hangar erupted into a 500-foot-high fireball, destroying a brand new Zeppelin Z9 inside. Both pilots were awarded the Distinguished Service Order for the actions.

The Zeppelin hangars at Friedrichshafen were the next target. Four Avro 504 biplanes, each carrying four 20lb bombs and piloted by Squadron Commander Featherstone-Briggs, Flight Commander Babington, Flight Lieutenant Sippe and Flight Sub Lieutenant Cannon, took off on 20 November 1914 from Belfort. Cannon's Avro developed engine trouble during take-off but the other three took off successfully and carried out the raid, causing damage to the hangars and Zeppelin Z7. Two Avros returned to Belfort, Featherstone-Briggs being shot down and taken prisoner. Shortly afterwards, due to the German Army advancing, the RNAS had to retire to a new base at Dunkirk while the German Air Service established their first base at Zeebrugge.

Although a great deal of attention was being given to shipboard aircraft at this time, the development of the flying boat was forging ahead. The idea was attractive – aircraft could take off and land from water without being shipboard. Because of his expertise in flying boats, a John Porte was commissioned with the rank of Squadron Commander in the Royal Flying Corps Naval Wing. In November 1914 the Admiralty purchased two American Curtiss flying boats and Porte reported on their use for service with the Royal Navy. Porte's report resulted in the Admiralty ordering sixty-two planes, designated as the Curtiss H.4 flying boat. These aircraft saw operational service throughout the war and proved extremely worthy.

The RNAS aircraft first used in raids had been deployed from land bases but on 24 December 1914 the Royal Navy changed tactics. The aircraft carriers HMS *Engadine*, *Empress* and *Riviera*, with a strong escort of two cruisers, eight destroyers and ten submarines, left Harwich at dusk and by 0530 hours on Christmas morning were stationed off the Frisian coast. The target was the Zeppelin hangars at Nordholz and the first naval air operation from carriers was underway.

HMA C.4 at RNAS Airship Station, Longside, Aberdeen, leaving to go on patrol.

At dawn seven RNAS seaplanes were airborne from the three carriers and headed for their target. Flying over the moored German fleet, the aircraft observers recorded as much detail as they could amid a barrage of enemy fire. Unable to reach the Zeppelin hangars the RNAS bombed as best they could but with little result. Of the seven aircraft that took off only two managed to get back to their aircraft carrier. The remainder ditched in the sea, with three of the crews being picked up by the British submarine E-11.

Stung by the raid, the German Kaiser ordered retaliatory Zeppelin air raids on England. Zeppelins L3, L4 and L6 attacked the east coast of England, killing and wounding civilians. The RNAS attempted to intercept the raids but their aircraft could not reach the Zeppelins' superior operating height. However, on 7 June 1915 the RNAS scored a major success over the Zeppelins. Flying a Morane-Saulnier Type L, No.3253, Flight Sub Lieutenant Rex Warneford managed to attack and destroy Zeppelin LZ37. For this action Warneford was awarded the Victoria Cross. Regretfully, he died in an aircraft accident ten days later.

The Dardanelles campaign of 1915 brought the RNAS aircraft of the Royal Navy to the fore. Winston Churchill, First Sea Lord, ordered HMS Ark Royal, with eight seaplanes aboard, to Mudros. Commander C.R. Samson, RNAS, was posted from Dunkirk with a makeshift squadron of men and aircraft to a rudimentary airstrip at Tenedos to support the intended Gallipoli landings. Soon the squadron was operational, carrying out bombing runs on the Turks. The ill-fated Gallipoli landings began on 18 March 1915 but HMS Ark Royal's aircraft were not airborne until an hour after Zero Hour. Commander Samson, flying overhead, could only watch helplessly as the invading Allied soldiers were slaughtered in the water.

The converted Isle of Man packet Ben-My-Chree, which had a flying-off deck and carried two prototype Short 184s, was soon also in action against the Turks. On 12 August 1915 one of the Short 184s, equipped with a 14in Whitehead torpedo and flown by Flight Commander C.H.K. Edmonds, attacked a Turkish supply ship and scored a direct torpedo hit amidships. This was the first time a ship had been attacked by an aircraft-dropped torpedo. A few days later a similar attack, carried out by Flight Lieutenant G.B. Dacre in another Short 184, sank a Turkish tug.

The Royal Flying Corps (RFC) took over the air defence of Britain – thereby releasing the RNAS to deal with the Imperial German Navy's seaplanes in the North Sea and English Channel. A single seat fighter, the Type C Bristol Scout, entered service with the RNAS for this purpose. The Scout had a service ceiling of 15,000 feet but a limited endurance of only two and a half hours. Sixty Scouts were in service with the RNAS by the beginning of 1916.

The limited endurance of the Bristol Scout restricted its use against Zeppelins: the Scout pilot had to catch the Zeppelin over the sea on its low-level approach before it climbed on its bombing run. To solve this problem, another converted Isle of Man packet, *Viking*, was renamed HMS *Vindex* and fitted with a 64ft deck for aircraft take-off only – landing had to be made on land. On 3 November 1915, in Harwich harbour, Flt Lt H.F. Towers took off from HMS *Vindex* in Bristol Scout No.1255. The first take-off from a ship by a landplane had been successful and a safe landing was made at RFC Martlesham Heath. The only alternative to heading for land was to ditch alongside the mother ship – strangely this was echoed by the Hurricane merchant-ship fighter of the Second World War, which had the same limited options. Bigger aircraft carriers were needed if they were to act as floating airfields – capable of carrying landplanes for both take-off and landing. The 20,000 ton Cunard liner *Campania* was therefore converted into a carrier, with a 200ft flying deck and hangarage for ten seaplanes: three Short 184s and seven Sopwiths.

The airship was still favoured by the Admiralty, mainly because of its longer endurance. Trying to get the best of both worlds, experiments were carried out with a BE2a slung underneath an airship. The idea was that the airship would carry the BE2a aloft then release it as required. On 21 February 1916 an experiment was carried out at RNAS Kingsnorth, Kent, in which an aircraft, piloted by Lieutenant Commander de Courcy-Ireland and Commander Usborne, was slung under S.S. Airship AP1. The airship lifted off but the locking clamps holding the aircraft to the airship malfunctioned at height. The aircraft fell away and both pilots were killed in the subsequent crash.

This experiment notwithstanding, the Naval Airship Service was to prove invaluable during the war. Great Britain, being an island, depended on sea traffic; naval airships provided aerial cover against German submarines and escorted convoys. The first anti-submarine coastal patrols were carried out on 10 August 1914 by two airships, His Majesty's Airship No. 3 (the

A Short 827 on service in East Africa.

RNAS officers being presented with awards by King George V during his visit to the Belgian Front early in 1916.

French-designed Astra Torres) and HMA No.4 (the former German-designed Parseval 18) in aerial support of the British Expeditionary Force when it crossed the Channel to France. These two airships patrolled the Channel for the first month of the war in 12-hour shifts. Later, airships continued to prove invaluable in patrolling the seas and protecting convoys from U-boat attack.

Late in 1915 No.3 Squadron RNAS was heavily engaged in bombing the Turks on the Turkish/Bulgarian border when one of the Squadron Commanders, Richard Bell-Davies, flying a single seat Nieuport 12 No.3172, landed amid enemy fire and rescued a downed pilot. This action earned him the Victoria Cross.

The Battle of Jutland on 31 May 1916 proved to be the first major sea battle in which aircraft were used. Vice Admiral Beatty, aboard HMS *Lion* ordered HMS *Engadine* to send out an aircraft to find the German fleet. A two-seat Short 184 No.8359, flown by Flight Lieutenant F.J. Rutland with Assistant Paymaster G.S. Trewin as observer, took off at 3.08 p.m. and located the enemy at 3.18 p.m. Observer Trewin radioed back to *Engadine* the disposition, speed and course of the German battleships amid a barrage of enemy anti-aircraft fire which was bracketing their aircraft. Rutland and Trewin returned to *Engadine* and found that their W/T messages had been received. The RNAS had proved their worth but, as the weather closed in, *Engadine* took no further part in the battle.

On land the Imperial German Air Service was more than holding its own against the RFC and the RNAS. The Fokker single-seat fighters outmatched the Allied fighters. In response, the Sopwith Aviation Company at Kingston-on-Thames produced two new aircraft types – Type 9700 (Sopwith $1\frac{1}{2}$ Strutter) and Type 9901 (Sopwith Pup).

The two-seat fighter/bomber $1\frac{1}{2}$ Strutter had a .303in machine gun with Sopwith-Kauper interrupter gear. Powered by a 130hp Clerget engine giving a speed of 106mph, it could carry two 65lb bombs and had a $4\frac{1}{2}$ hour endurance. The rear cockpit observer had a .303in Lewis on

Short 184 No.N1616 on the beach at Calshot. Note the two bombs under the forward part of the fuselage.

a Scarff ring. Over 550 Sopwith 1½ Strutters were supplied to the RNAS for use as a landplane, the first coming into service with No.5 Wing in April 1916.

The Sopwith Pup was a single-seat fighter which could be shipborne. Powered by a 80hp Le Rhone engine it had a top speed of 111mph and could climb and fight up to 17,000 feet. It was armed with a single Lewis gun firing forward or eight Le Prieur rockets mounted on the struts. The Pup could out-manoeuvre the German Albatross although the latter had a larger engine. In September 1916 No.1 (Naval) Wing at Dunkirk was the first RNAS fighter wing to receive the Sopwith Pup. Within days the Sopwiths were in action when Flt Sub Lieutenant S.J. Goble engaged a German LVG bomber in his Pup and brought it down in flames.

By the autumn of 1916, the RFC was suffering badly at the hands of the German Imperial Air Service and petitioned the Admiralty for assistance in their air battles. Accordingly, No. 8 (Naval) Squadron was formed and based at Vert Galand, France. The 'Naval Eight' as it became known, had three flights equipped with six Sopwith Pups, six Sopwith 1½ Strutters and six Nieuports. By the year's end they had shot down twenty German aircraft.

Another Squadron, No. 10 (Naval), was formed later and B Flight, made up of Canadian pilots, was led by Flight Sub Lieutenant Raymond Collishaw (later to become Air Vice Marshal Collishaw). B Flight flew Sopwith Triplanes and became known as 'Black Flight' as their aircraft were named *Black Death*, *Black Maria*, *Black Prince*, *Black Rodger* and *Black Sheep*. Between May and July 1917 the Flight shot down eighty-seven German aircraft with Collishaw being credited with sixteen victories during a twenty-seven-day period. By the end of the war Collishaw had downed sixty aircraft, making him the third highest ace behind Mannock (73) and Bishop (72).

A new type of airship appeared in April 1917, the N.S. (North Sea) 1. It was the last of the non-rigid airships of the First World War and only sixteen were built. The N.S. 1 was larger than any other British airship with an overall length of 262 feet and endurance of twenty-one hours. A crew of ten was carried in an enclosed cabin slung under the airship. In May 1917 the 'Little America' Curtiss H.4 flying boats already in use were joined by the larger Curtiss H.12. Named the 'Large America', the H.12 had a crew of two pilots and four air gunners. Two 230lb

A Sopwith Camel of the RNAS upside down after a landing accident.

bombs were carried beneath the wings.

A new aircraft patrol system, 'Spiders Web', was introduced on 1 May 1917, with the Curtiss H.12 flying the first of these anti-submarine and anti-Zeppelin patrols. Success soon followed when on 14 May 1917 Curtiss H.12 No.8666, flown by Flt Lt Galpin, intercepted and shot down Zeppelin L.22. On 14 June Curtiss H.12 No.8677, flown by Flt Lt Hobbs, shot down Zeppelin L.42. The Zeppelin had met its match.

The Curtiss H.12s also had great success against U-boats. On 20 May 1917 Flt Lts Morrish and Boswell sighted the surfaced UC-36 in the North Sea. They attacked and sank the U-Boat – the first submarine to be sunk by a flying boat. A month later two H.12s, Nos. 8662 and 8676, caught the surfaced UB-20 in the North Sea and bombed as the submarine dived. On 28 September 1917 Flt Lts Hobbs and Dickey claimed the sinking of the UC-6.

By June 1917 the 22,500 ton aircraft carrier HMS *Furious* was commissioned. Three Short 184 seaplanes with folding wings and five Sopwith Pups with non-folding wings were on the carrier's complement.

Taking off from *Furious* caused few problems – but landing did, the flight deck being just 228ft long by 50ft wide. On 2 August 1917, trials were made to effect a landing with *Furious* steaming ahead at 25 knots. Sopwith Pup No.N6452, flown by Squadron Commander Dunning, was fitted with rope toggles under each wing, the intent being that deck crew could grab the toggles, hang on and stop the aircraft. Dunning took off in the Pup and circled *Furious* then made his landing run. As he touched down the toggles were seized and held by the deck crew. Dunning stopped the engine and got out, becoming the first pilot to land an aircraft on a moving ship.

A second successful landing was made on the 7 August 1917. However, Dunning wanted to repeat his success immediately and took off again. This time the Pup engine stalled on touchdown and the aircraft, caught by a strong, sudden gust of wind, cartwheeled over the side into the sea. Dunning was trapped in the cockpit and drowned before he could be rescued. Landings were then banned on *Furious* for the time being.

Further take-off experiments were carried out on HMS *Yarmouth* and Lt F.J. Rutland successfully flew off a Sopwith Pup on 10 June 1917. Real success came on 21 August 1917 when Flt Sub Lt B.A. Smart made his first take-off from HMS *Yarmouth* on operations in the

Sopwith Pup No.6183 *Mildred H* of No. 3 (Naval) Squadron with the pilot, Squadron Commander Lloyd Breadner, in the cockpit and two members of his ground crew.

North Sea. *Yarmouth* was being shadowed by Zeppelin L-23 at 8000 feet when Smart took off, climbed to 9000 feet, then attacked and destroyed the L-23. Smart landed his Pup in the sea and was safely picked up. This was the first time a Zeppelin had been shot down by a fighter from a moving warship. The RNAS had fully gained its spurs.

By the end of March 1918 RNAS strength had increased in just four years from a handful of aircraft to 2949 planes, 103 airships and 67,000 officers and men manning 126 naval air stations. Flying boats and seaplanes continued to make their contribution until the end of the war and were used extensively for submarine-hunting, communication and observation flights. On occasions they carried out convoy protection duties and a number of German submarines were either sunk or badly damaged. S.S.(Sea Scout), S.S.Z., Coastal, C* (Star) and N.S. (North Sea) airships carried out observation flights and convoy protection duties in the North Sea, English Channel and Western Approaches. Their vigilance during the convoy patrols was instrumental in saving numerous lives and ensuring that the merchant ships were able to bring supplies to Britain without interference from the German U-boats. Meanwhile, in France, the Royal Naval Air Service squadrons accounted for a fair share of the victories against the German Air Service and without question played a major part in the eventual victory of the Allies.

On 1 April the RNAS was combined with the RFC into the Royal Air Force. Ex-RN officers who transferred to the new RAF were given their equivalent in Army ranks (RAF ranks as such were not introduced until 1920). In four years, the Royal Naval Air Service had established itself within the framework of the British Military Forces as a service that could hold its own globally.

One
The Early Years

The first British airship, *Nulli Secundus*, at Farnborough in 1907.

The Vickers Naval Rigid Airship No.1 *Mayfly*, approaching her mooring post on Cavendish Dock, Barrow-in-Furness, on 22 May 1911.

Previous page: Hall's Flying School at Hendon, just before the First World War. This was a one of a number of flying schools that trained pilots prior to their joining either the RFC or the RNAS.

HMA No.1 is seen here with her back broken after being caught by a gust of wind whilst being backed out of her hangar. She never flew.

Mayfly again, showing the twisted damage to its framework after the accident in Barrow-in-Furness on 22 May 1911.

After the *Mayfly* fiasco the Royal Navy concentrated on planes, but airships continued to be manufactured for service. Here, the airship *Parseval* is being moved into its hangar at Farnborough in February 1914.

The very early days of the RNAS seen here with Flight Sub Lieutenant Le Mesurier in the cockpit of a Bleriot, one of the first aircraft in the RNAS.

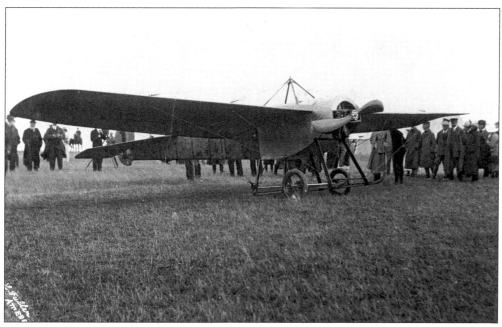

A Hanriot Monoplane is seen here at Larkhill during the military trials.

The First Lord of the Admiralty, Winston Churchill, after his first flight in an aeroplane.

The Avro D Biplane, powered by a 35hp Green engine. It is seen here after being fitted with floats and taken to Cavendish Dock, Barrow-in-Furness, where on 18 November 1911 it took to the air after several unsuccessful attempts, becoming the first British aircraft to take off from water.

Evaluation trials at RNAS Yarmouth in 1913 involving a Short S.41.

An early Sopwith seaplane with wheeled floats and short folding wings at Calshot.

A Sopwith Tractor on trials in the Solent. It was powered by a 100hp Anzani engine.

Commander C.R. Samson in his Short S.41 at Dover on 13 July 1912 during a flight from Portsmouth to Harwich. Samson was in the process of evaluating aircraft for the Royal Navy.

A Maurice Farman floatplane, No.95, powered by a 130hp Canton-Unne engine, is seen here at Felixstowe in August 1914.

A Short S.41 about to take off from the Harbour at Weymouth, Dorset.

A student pilot in an F.B.A (Franco British Aviation) flying boat with his instructor on the left at Calshot, Southampton on 1 September 1917.

HMS *Hibernia* with a Short S.27 on her launching ramp during the trials in Weymouth Bay.

HMS *Hibernia* in Weymouth Bay, Dorset, in May 1912 with two aircraft on her launching ramp – an S.38 and an S.41. These were amongst the first trials of launching aircraft from ships.

Lt Charles Rumney Samson in January 1912 about to take off from HMS *Africa* in a Short S.27 to carry out the first flight from a British warship.

Eugene Ely landing aboard the American cruiser USS *Pennsylvania* on 18 January 1911. This was the first landing of an aircraft on a ship.

Two
War at Sea

The German cruiser S.M.S. *Königsberg* leaving Dar-es-Salaam.

A Curtiss Model F Flying boat at Simons Bay, Cape, South Africa, in November 1914. This aircraft, together with its civilian pilot, Mr Cutler, was requisitioned by the Royal Navy and used as an observation aircraft in the *Königsberg* incident.

Previous page: A Short Admiralty Type 827 floatplane. This photograph was taken as the aircraft left the factory, hence the pristine condition.

The S.M.S. *Königsberg* spotted from the air by Flt Lt J.T. Cull, RNAS, from a height of 700ft on 25 April 1915.

An aerial shot of HMS *Newbridge* blocking the channel in the Rufigi River.

HMS *Newbridge* after being sunk as a blockade ship in the Rufigi Delta to prevent the *Königsberg* from escaping.

Unpacking one of the Caudron aircraft from its case, at the entrance to the Rufigi Delta.

Flt Lt J.T. Cull.

HMS *Chatham* firing her guns at the S.M.S. *Königsberg*.

The wrecked German cruiser after her guns had been removed.

HMS *Hermes* sinking in the English Channel after being torpedoed in October 1914.

The original aircraft carrier HMS *Ark Royal*.

The converted seaplane carrier HMS *Engadine*.

The converted seaplane carrier HMS *Riviera*.

The converted seaplane carrier HMS *Empress*.

The seaplane carrier HMS *Ark Royal*.

The converted seaplane carrier HMS *Ben-My-Chree*.

The converted seaplane carrier HMS *Manxman*.

A Sopwith Baby being hoisted aboard HMS *Riviera*.

Loading Short 184 No.N9290 on board HMS *Pegasus*, bound for Russia in 1919.

The aircraft carrier HMS *Argus*.

A seaplane being taken from its hangar aboard HMS *Ark Royal*.

The converted seaplane carrier HMS *Campania*.

Seven Sopwith Pups on the
228ft deck of HMS *Furious*.

Sopwith 2F1 Camels aboard
the aircraft carrier HMS
Furious in 1918.

Sopwith Pup No.N6454 being hoisted onto the deck of HMS *Furious*. Note the extremely restricted opening onto the hangar deck below – it can be measured in inches.

Sopwith 2F1 Camel No.N6603, flown by Flt Lt Tomlinson, RNAS, taking off from the flight deck of HMS *Pegasus* (formerly the Great Eastern Railway steamer *Stockholm*).

Sopwith 2F1 Camel No.N6603. This aircraft served aboard HMS *Pegasus*; HMS *Tiger* and HMAS *Melbourne* carrying out a series of landing and take-off trials.

An excellent overhead shot of a Sopwith 2F1 Camel on the 'flight deck' of an unknown cruiser. What is clearly shown is the restricted length of the deck for take-off.

A Sopwith 2F1 Camel taking off from the deck of HMS *Pegasus*.

A Camel taking off from the deck of HMS *Vindex* during trials.

Another Sopwith 2F1 Camel taking off from the deck of what is probably HMS *Nairana*.

HMS *Calliope*, again with a Sopwith 2F1 Camel.

A close-up of a the undercarriage configuration of a Sopwith 2F1 Camel with grappling hooks fitted to the main undercarriage bar together with an air-screw guard.

A Sopwith Pup leaving HMS *Malaya*, flown by Lt Eric Breed. It is interesting to note how the 'flight deck' was mounted on top of the gun barrels.

A Sopwith 2F1 Camel aboard HMS *Royal Sovereign*, showing the damage caused by the violent reverberations of the ship's 15-inch guns when they were fired.

No, not an aircraft crashing, but Sopwith F1 Camel No.B3878 on ditching trials on 9 August 1918.

An aerial shot of a lighter with a Sopwith F1 Camel on the deck.

An RNAS lighter being prepared for take off trials using the Sopwith F1 Camel. Note the drawing of the Camel on the deck of the lighter.

Sopwith 2F1 Camel No.N6623, fitted with skids and flown by Cmdr C.R. Samson, on a lighter at Felixstowe on 29 May 1918. These were the first trials of taking off from the deck of the lighter.

Another Sopwith F1 Camel flown by Lt S.D. Culley being towed out to sea on a lighter on 31 July 1918 for take-off trials.

Lt S.D. Culley, in his Sopwith F1 Camel, takes off successfully from the towed lighter.

A close-up of the deck-landing skids on Flt Sub Lt Dickson's Sopwith Pup during deck-landing trials on 15 April 1918, showing the central arrester hook.

Sopwith Pup No.N6452 being transported by pontoon out to HMS *Furious* at Scapa Flow for deck-landing trials.

Squadron Commander E.H. Dunning landing on HMS *Furious* on his first attempt. Fellow pilots and deck crew rush forward to grab the aircraft and pull it down onto the deck.

Sqdn Cdr Dunning embarking in his Sopwith Pup to take off for his second and fatal deck landing.

Dunning touches down on the deck of HMS *Furious* during his second attempt. The deck crew scramble to get hold of the aircraft.

Squadron Commander Dunning's plane is caught by a sudden gust of wind and is blown over the side before any of the deck crews can catch hold of the aircraft.

The wreckage of Dunning's Sopwith Pup being hauled from the water after the accident, with his body still inside the cockpit.

The wreckage of the Pup stands on the deck of HMS *Furious* after being recovered from the sea.

A Blackburn Baby taxiing toward the slipway at RNAS Killingholme.

Short 184 No.N4393, powered by a 320hp Sunbeam Cossack engine, prepares to carry out torpedo trials off Calshot on 19 February 1918.

Short 184 No.N4393, dropping its Whitehead torpedo during the trials.

This photograph, taken after release of the torpedo, highlights the danger of dropping the torpedo whilst flying close to the surface of the water. The splash from the torpedo can clearly be seen reaching the underside of the fuselage of the aircraft.

Sopwith T. Cuckoo No.N6966, dropping a Whitehead torpedo during trials.

A Wight built AD 1000 carrying out torpedo trials off Calshot, Southampton.

Sopwith Baby No.N1063, powered by a 110hp Clerget engine, on the slipway at RNAS Dundee in February 1918. The pilot, Lt V.D. Grant, was about to attempt to fly under the Tay Bridge.

The remains of Lt Grant's attempt to fly his Sopwith Baby under the Tay Bridge.

Sopwith Baby No.N1413, built by Blackburn for anti-Zeppelin duties.

An Eastchurch-built Short Type 830 in a folded configuration, being transported along a road.

The original Short 184 being lowered into the water at Rochester in 1915. The Short is seen in its earliest form, with upper-plane, single-acting ailerons only.

FBA (Franco British Aviation) No.3642 on the slipway at RNAS Killingholme in 1916.

Short prototype 310-A at Rochester in July 1916, with an 18in Whitehead Mk.IX 1000lb torpedo slung beneath the fuselage. The figure on the far right of the picture is Oswald Short, the plane's designer.

Sopwith Schneider No.3768 upside down in the water after a landing accident at RNAS Killingholme in 1916.

Here, the Schneider has come to rest further up the beach.

Sopwith Schneider No.3768 on the slipway at RNAS Killingholme after its recovery from the beach.

The Robey-built Short 184 No.N2833, powered by a 225hp Sunbeam engine, on its beaching trolley at RNAS Calshot in 1917.

A Wight Type A1 seaplane being hoisted aboard HMS *Ark Royal* at the Dardanelles in 1915.

The Wight-built AD 1000 No.1358 in the water off Calshot.

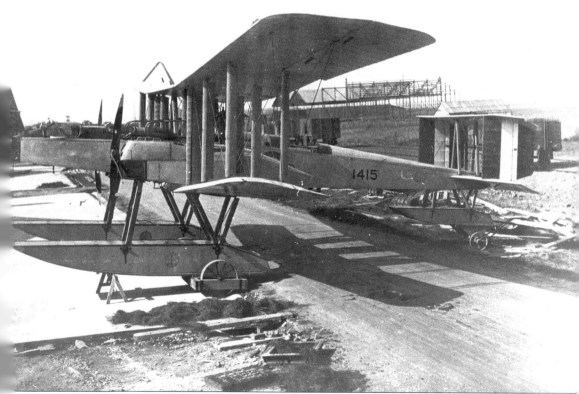

Blackburn GP seaplane No.1415 on its beaching trolley.

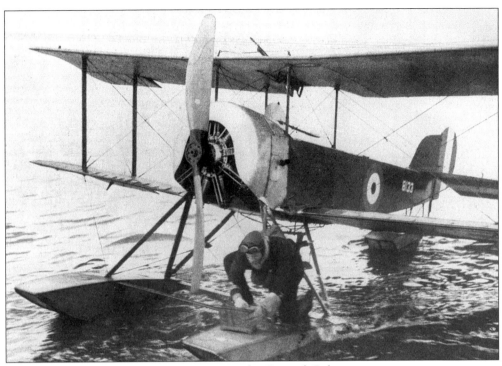

An RNAS pilot carries out running repairs on his Sopwith Baby.

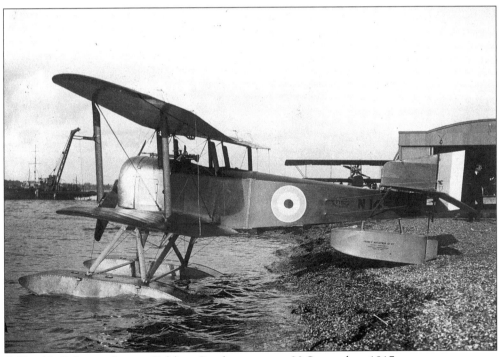

A Hamble Baby seaplane at Calshot, Southampton on 20 September, 1917.

Sopwith Schneider No.8210 on its beaching trolley at RNAS Calshot.

The Hamble Baby seaplane was powered by a 130hp Clerget engine and fitted with a synchronised Lewis gun.

Sopwith Bat Boat No.1 on taxiing trials.

A Robey-built Short 184, No.N1274, powered by a 240hp Mercedes engine, being pushed out into the water at RNAS Calshot prior to a test flight.

Unfolding the wings of a Wight converted seaplane – powered by a Sunbeam Maori engine –
prior to its launch at Calshot on 5 December 1917.

A standard Wight converted seaplane in folded configuration on the slipway at RNAS Calshot
after a test flight.

Blackburn Baby floatplane No.N2071. Note the 112lb bomb under the fuselage and the two stripped Lewis guns, one mounted on the upper wing and one mounted on the engine cowling in front of the pilot.

Curtiss H.12 'Large America' No.8681 anchored off RNAS Killingholme.

A Curtiss H.4 'Small America' being prepared for launching.

A 'Baby America' with Bristol Scout C No.3028 on the upper wing. This was an early experiment in 'parasite' fighter protection.

A Felixstowe F.3 Fury being eased down the slipway and into the water at Malta.

A Short 'Dover' Type about to be lowered into the water off Rochester for the first time.

A Curtiss-Wanamaker Triplane. These aircraft were brought over from the USA and assembled in England.

A film crew in a Short 184 aboard HMS *Ben-My-Chree* at Salonika in 1916.

Curtiss H.4 'Small America' No.1232, on its launching trolley at RNAS Killingholme.

Felixstowe F2A No.N4545 in dazzle camouflage while on patrol over the North Sea.

The cockpit of the Felixstowe F.2A.

Supermarine Baby No. N59 on its launching trolley on the Isle of Grain on 1 May 1918.

A Standard Wight converted seaplane powered by a Rolls-Royce Eagle engine, about to take off on a test flight from RNAS Calshot.

Handley Page R/200 seaplane No.N23. This was one of only three built for the RNAS.

The Blackburn Blackburd (*sic*) N113, the first of just three examples built as ship-borne torpedo-bombers.

Three
War on Land

Avro 504s of the RNAS, about to take off from Belfort Airfield, France, to raid the Zeppelin sheds at Friedrichshafen.

Flt Cmdr Babington and Flt Lt Sippe of the RNAS, being decorated with the Legion of Honour and the Cross of the Order by General Thévnet, the governor of the Fortress of Belfort, for their part in the raid on the Zeppelin sheds at Friedrichshafen.

Previous page: Officers and men of No. 1 Wing, RNAS, with a 'highly secret experimental fighter aircraft' at Dunkerque airfield in 1915.

Flt Sub Lts Mulock and Beard of No.1 Wing, RNAS, about to take off in their Nieuport fighters for a bombing sortie against Zeppelin sheds at Evere, near Brussels, in 1915. Each aircraft carried six 20lb Hales bombs beneath the fuselage.

Flight Commander W. Bigsworth of No.1 Wing, RNAS at Dunkirk, standing in front of his Avro 504B, No.1009, in which he attacked a Zeppelin over Ostend at 0405 hours on 17 May 1915. He was later awarded the DSO for the attack.

A Turkish 6in shell bursting near the RNAS airfield on Long Island in the Gulf of Smyrna, East Mediterranean. The hangar in the foreground is that of No.2 Wing, RNAS, with a Henry Farman, a Nieuport and a dummy aircraft in the making, near the hangar entrance. When the dummy was completed it was placed in the centre of the airfield. The Turks fired over seventy rounds at it and never even came close to hitting it.

Turkish POWs were taken under armed escort to help clear the RNAS airfields at Gallipoli in 1915.

An RNAS crew about to set off on patrol in a French Breguet bomber in the spring of 1915. The figure in black with his back to the camera on the right of the group is the aircraft's designer M. Breguet.

A Handley Page 0/100 bomber of No. 7(N) Squadron, approaching Couderkerque on 5 June 1917 with HM King Albert of Belgium aboard. The King's head can be seen on the left of the picture.

Sopwith 1½ Strutter *Elsie* V, with her crew in front.

Flt Lt K. Savory and Flt Sub Lt Dickenson with the BE2c in which they bombed Constantinople.

The crew-room mess of No. 5 Wing, RNAS.

The No. 5(N) Squadron intelligence room at Petite Synthe.

Members of the armament section of No.214 Squadron, RNAS at Dunkirk, arming bombs prior to a raid on 1 June 1918.

RNAS ground crew with the remains of a crashed BE2c spread over three lorries.

Sopwith Pup No.6209 of No. 3(N) Squadron makes a somewhat unorthodox landing.

Lanchester Armoured Car No. 4 of A Section, No.15 Squadron, RNAS.

The prototype Sopwith Triplane, No.N500, with A Squadron, RNAS, at Furnes for trials in June 1916.

Sopwith Triplane No.N5438 of No.1 Squadron, RNAS, flown by Flt Sub Lt C.A. Eyre.

Sopwith Triplanes of No. 1(N) Squadron lined up ready for inspection in 1917.

J.A. Shaw's Sopwith Triplane of No. 8(N) Squadron in 1917.

This Fairey Hamble Baby, flown by Flight Commander E.A. de Ville and used by the RNAS on coastal and anti-submarine patrols, had the misfortune of running into this wireless mast at Horsey Island, Portsmouth. The pilot managed to clamber down and after a great deal of dangerous work the aircraft was recovered.

A landing accident involving two Sopwith 1½ Strutters of No.3 Wing, RNAS.

Sopwith 1F1 Camel No.B3834 *Wonga Bonga* of No. 12(N) Squadron, in which Flt Sub Lt Brandon shot down a Gotha bomber on 22 August 1917.

Sopwith 1½ Strutters of No.5 Wing, RNAS, at Coudekerque airfield in November 1916, preparing for a daylight sortie.

Nieuport 17b No.N3204 of No. 6(N) Squadron, RNAS. The aircraft was lost on 6 June 1917, when it was shot down by Vzfw. Riesinger of Jasta 12. The pilot, Flt Sub Lt F.P. Reeves was killed.

German soldiers recovering a Sopwith 1F1 Camel after it was shot down by ground fire on 10 March 1918. The pilot, Flt Sub Lt K.D. Campbell, survived the crash landing and was made a POW.

Wreckage of Sopwith F1 Camel No.B3868 of No. 1(N) Squadron at Manston after ground-looping on landing.

Gunnery practice for trainee pilots on a 'sophisticated' piece of equipment.

A modified Sopwith 2F1 Camel, fitted with twin Vickers machine guns and a jettisonable undercarriage, undergoing trials at Felixstowe. The aircraft is parked beneath the wing of a Felixstowe Fury flying boat, giving an excellent indication of both the small size of the Camel and the enormity of the Felixstowe Fury.

The prototype Sopwith Triplane No.N500 is seen here before being handed over to the RNAS.

Sopwith Camels of No. 3(N) Squadron at Middle Airfield, Dunkirk, in February 1918.

Sopwith 1F1 Camels of No.8(N) Squadron at Mont St Eloi in March 1918.

Sopwith F1 Camel No.B3926 *Happy Hawkins*, flown by D.M. Galbraith but seen here with Capt. McD. Allan.

A captured Sopwith 1F1 Camel, formerly of No.3(N) Squadron, in German markings at Epinoy airfield, the home of Jasta 23b, in May 1918. Otto Kissenberth, later awarded the coveted Pour le Mérite, was flying this aircraft when he shot down an SE5a on 16May 1918 at Tilloy. It was his twentieth victory.

Sopwith 1½ Strutters of No. 3 Wing, RNAS, at Luxeuil in 1917.

Nieuport 17b C1 No.N3204 of No. 6(N) Squadron. This aircraft was later destroyed when it was shot down on 6 June 1917 by Vzfw. Riesinger of Jasta 12, killing the pilot, Flt Lt F.P. Reeves.

A Sopwith Pup, with a top-wing-mounted Lewis machine gun, about to take off on patrol from RNAS Yarmouth.

DH4s of No.2 Squadron, RNAS, at Bergues, France, in March 1918.

DH4 No.N6000 B1 of No. 5(N) Squadron at Petite Synthe airfield, Dunkirk, in 1917. This was the usual machine of Flt Lt C.P.O. Bartlett of B Flight. RNAS DH4s differed from the RFC versions in having two Vickers machine guns for the pilot.

Sopwith Pup No.N6171, of No. 3(N) Squadron at Marieux, France, upside down after the airfield was hit by severe gales.

Sopwith Pup *Julia* at RNAS Walmer in 1918. The pilot, Flt Sub Lt J.A. Shaw can be seen standing by the tail.

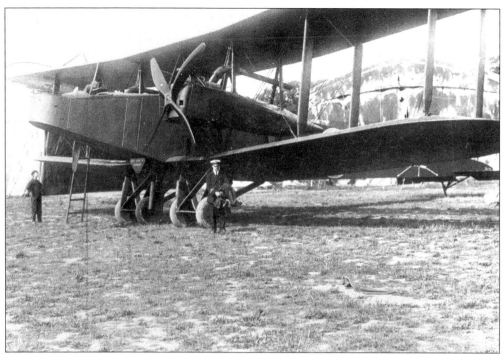

Handley Page 0/100 bomber No.3117 at Manston. Note the large tented hangar in the background.

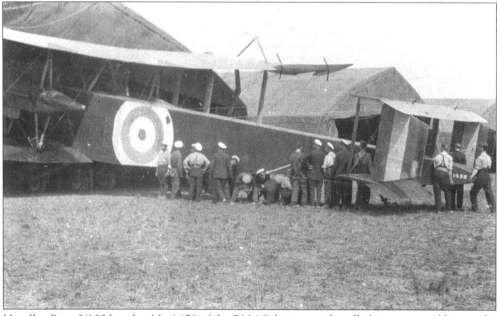

Handley Page 0/100 bomber No.1458 of the RNAS, being manhandled into a tented hangar for servicing.

Handley Page 0/100 bomber No.1459 *Le Tigre* of No.3 Wing, RNAS at Ochey, France, in March 1917. This was the first 0/100 bomber to land in France.

Another view of Handley Page 0/100 bomber No.1459 at Ochey. Note the unusual camouflage on the underside of the aircraft.

Handley Page 0/400 bomber No.D9702 *Clayton*, with two members of the crew standing in front.

RNAS maintenance ground crew servicing a Handley Page 0/400 bomber of 214 Squadron, RAF, at Dunkirk on 1 June 1918.

The first Handley Page 0/100 bomber to land at Coudekerque on 4 March 1917. The crew were Squadron Commander D.A. Spenser-Grey, Flt Sub Lt Barker, Flt Sub Lt St John and WO Polly.

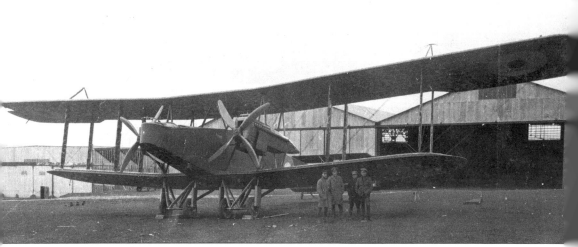

Handley Page 0/100 No.1459 of No. 3(N) Wing at Ochey, France, in March 1917.

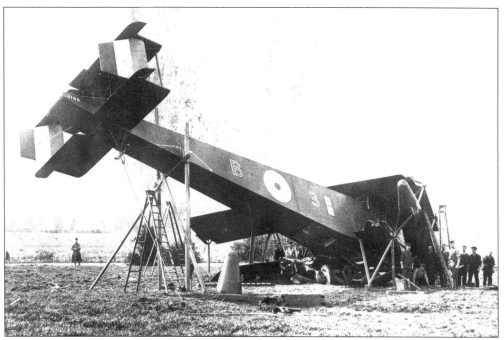

Recovering the wreckage of Handley Page 0/100 bomber No.3135 B-3 of No.5 Wing, RNAS, which crashed at Coudekerque on 30 July 1918.

The wreckage of Handley Page 0/100 bomber A-3 of No.7(N) Squadron, which crashed at Coudekerque on 11 December 1917, in the process of being recovered.

The wreckage of Handley Page 0/100 bomber A-3 of No. 7(N) Squadron, in the process of being righted.

Short bomber No.9491 drops in unexpectedly on the headquarters at Coudekerque on 29 April 1917. The pilot, Flt Sub Lt Sands, survived the crash and there were no injuries. This shot was taken from the top of a hangar.

Short bomber No.9491 after crashing into the headquarters buildings.

This picture shows the extensive damage to the bomber.

The Astra Torres airship at Farnborough.

A Coastal Class airship, C.23a, from RNAS Mullion in Cornwall, escorts an Allied convoy in the Western Approaches.

Previous page: Royal Naval Airship C.23A about to take off on patrol. These patrolling airships were extremely successful in dissuading enemy submarines from attacking the Allied convoys.

The view from the gondola of an N.S. (North Sea) airship while on merchant convoy patrol in the Western Approaches.

Not all the airship patrols were uneventful and successful. Here, Coastal Airship C.27 plummets into the North Sea in flames, after being destroyed by gunfire from a Brandenburg floatplane flown by Oberleutnant Friedrich Christiansen.

An RNAS airship taking off on patrol. Note the boat-shaped gondola slung beneath.

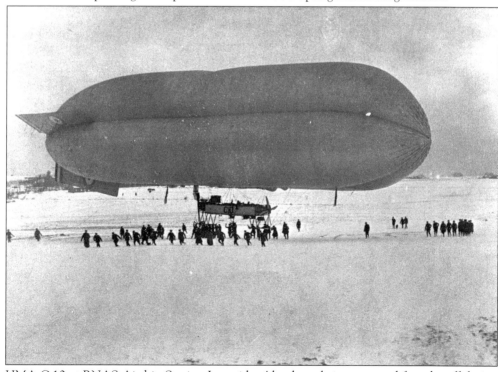

HMA C.10 at RNAS Airship Station Longside, Aberdeen, being prepared for take off during the winter.

An RNAS airship concealed in a coastal forest just prior to lifting off to go on patrol in the English Channel.

RNAS airship C.21 at Folkestone on 1 June 1918 after hitting a hut roof as it approached to land, resulting in a badly gashed envelope that caused the airship to collapse in the middle.

North Sea Airship N.S.9 taking off to go on patrol over the North Sea.

A kite balloon being winched down during tests at Roehampton.

On 21 February 1916, an experiment to carry an aircraft by airship was carried out at RNAS Kingsnorth, Kent. The aircraft, seen here suspended beneath the airship, A.P.1, was piloted by Lieutenant Commander de Courcy-Ireland and Commander Usborne. As the airship approached the dropping height, the locking clamps holding the aircraft malfunctioned. The plane fell away and, unable to control the aircraft, both pilots were killed in the subsequent crash.

Another experiment, at Pulham in November 1918, with a Sopwith 2F1 Camel, No.N6814, flown by Lt R.E.Keys, DFC, slung beneath HMA 23.

Five
The Men of the Hour

A public schoolboy off to war.

Officers on No.1 Wing, RNAS, comprising No. 2(N) and No. 3(N) Squadrons. From left to right, back row: -?-, -?-, Bette, Alexander, -?-, Nelson, Richardson, White, Wambolt, Beamish, Hosketh, Powell. Middle row: Wyatt, Mack, Smilie, McNab, Mulock, Wng Cmdr Chambers, Sqdn Cmdr Evill, Greenwood, Edwards, Furniss, Taylor. Front row: Gow, Chase, Travers, Holder, Tapscott, Griffen.

Previous page: Some officers of No.1 Wing, RNAS, in September 1915. From left to right, back row: Graham, Stoddart, Mulock, Holmes, Peal, Watson, Beard. Middle row: D'Albiac, Jackson, Bigsworth, Longmore, Haskins, Evill. Front row: Carew, Nutting, Furneval.

Flight Sub Lt Rex Warneford, VC.

J.A. Shaw in the cockpit of his Sopwith Pup, *Julia*, at Walmer in 1918.

Air crew of No.3 Wing, RNAS at Ochey, April 1917. From left to right, Flt Sub Lt J.F. Jones, Flt Sub Lt Hains, Lt Cmdr E.W. Stedman, Flt Sub Lt E.B. Waller, Flt Sub Lt D.R.C. Wright, Flt Sub Lt Pepperel, Flt Sub Lt Paul Bewasher.

Robinson and Cleaver's shop window in London, displaying the smart flying clothing that was on sale to officers of the RFC and RNAS.

Major Roderic Stanley Dallas, DSO, DSC, an Australian fighter 'Ace' credited with at least fifty-one victories, is seen here in fur flying clothing, leaning against the fuselage of Nieuport Scout No.3938 of No.1 Squadron, RNAS. Dallas was killed in action on 1 June 1918, when he was shot down by Ltn. Hans Werner of Jasta 14.

Major Roderic Dallas, DSO, DSC, in the cockpit of his SE5a, No.D3511 on 28 May 1918, three days before he was shot down and killed.

Air crew of No.3 Wing, RNAS, at Luxeuil-les-Bains in late 1916. Seated are Wing Captain W.L.Elder (on the left) and Squadron Commander R. Bell-Davies, VC. The remaining officers are Canadian.

The unglamorous side of being a fighter pilot in war. The body of an RNAS pilot lies beside his aircraft after being shot down. German soldiers crowd around ghoulishly.

No.203 Squadron personnel on 10 July 1918 on occasion of the visit of King George V to Izel-le-Hameau. From left to right, back row: F.T.S. Sehl, Fitzpatrick, Black, Stone, Nelson, Adams, Lick, Breakey, Rudge. Middle row: Louis D.Baulf, Art Whealey, Harold Beamish, Raymond Collishaw, Rochford, Haynes, Haig. Front row: Sidebottom, Carter, Hunter, Bingham, Townsend, Dixey, Duke.

Squadron Commander Raymond Collishaw, DSO, DFC, RNAS, talking with Lt A.T. Whealy of No.203 Squadron, RAF, at Allonville, France, in July 1918.

Squadron Commander Roderic Dallas and Flt Lt. Gerrard of No.1 (N) Squadron, RNAS, receiving French decorations at Furnes in 1917.

RNAS officers at Petite Synthe in 1917. They are, left to right, Le Mesurier, CPO Bartlett and Garrad.

RNAS officers at RNAS Yarmouth. In the centre is Lt Egbert Cadbury.

Three RNAS officers with an alternative form of transport.

Officers of No.5 (N) Squadron at Petite Synthe in 1917. From left to right, standing: Cleghorn, Pownhall, Sproatt, Goldsmith (IO), Potts (EO), Lupton, Wright, Mason, Ormerod, Dickson. Seated: Shaw, St John, Newton-Clare, Le Mesurier, Goble (CO), Clarke, Jope-Slade, CPO Bartlett.

Lt Eric Breed about to board his aircraft on HMS *Malaya.*

RNAS ground crew personnel with their Daimler lorry in France in 1916. Note the inscription on the side of the lorry, 'Fred Karno's Airmen'. We think this was their way of reflecting the chaos and lack of organisation that dogged them throughout the war.

RNAS ground crew relaxing with a cup of tea. The war was over.

RNAS personnel marching through London at the end of the war.